CHARLES RENNIE MACKINTOSH

RICHARD DREW
PUBLISHING
GLASGOW

(................ Annan c.1903)

First published in 1987 by
Richard Drew Publishing Ltd
6 Clairmont Gardens
Glasgow G3 7LW
Scotland

British Library
Cataloguing in Publication Data
Grigg, Jocelyn
Charles Rennie Mackintosh.
1. Mackintosh, Charles Rennie
2. Architects—Scotland
     —Biography
I. Title
720'.92'4   NA977.M3
ISBN 0-86267-191-4

Designed by
James W. Murray
Typeset in Paladium
by Fraser Ross at
Glasgow School of Art
Printed in Scotland by
Swains
(Edinburgh) Ltd

CONTENTS

Detail of Sitting Room Windows, The Hill House

CHARLES RENNIE MACKINTOSH 1868-1928

'THE CITY IN WHICH ONLY ENGINEERS PROSPER: RAW, RICH Glasgow'[1] was the home of Charles Rennie Mackintosh. Here he was born in 1868, trained as an architect and created almost all the buildings and interiors which won him enthusiastic acclaim on the Continent as a pioneer of modern architecture and design, but so little local recognition that he finally left his city in failure and died in London in total obscurity.

Mackintosh's Glasgow, prospering in its expanding commerce and industry, was the rapidly growing, self-satisfied and dirty 'Second City of the Empire', busy advertising its new wealth in ostentatious civic architecture, its prestige in enormous international exhibitions, and its industry in a great deal of grime and smog. Yet the City's prosperity also fostered a significant artistic renaissance at the end of the 19th century. Local businessmen, anxious to be seen as discerning patrons of the arts, collected the paintings of the 'Glasgow Boys' and furnished their homes in the distinctive 'Glasgow Style' created by a new generation of young designers. At the centre of a lively and progressive movement in the creative arts was the Glasgow School of Art, then flourishing under the brilliant direction of Francis Newbery.

As an assistant in the architects' office of Honeyman & Keppie, Mackintosh also attended evening drawing classes at the School, won prizes for a number of conventional competition designs and came to the attention of the young director and his wife. Newbery was not only responsible for Mackintosh's most important architectural commission—the new Glasgow School of Art—but he and Jessie remained his staunchest friends throughout his life. At the School Mackintosh and his friend and colleague Herbert MacNair also met the women they were to marry: the artist sisters Margaret and Frances Macdonald. 'The Four' collaborated on designs for furniture, metalwork and illustration, and after their marriage in 1900 Margaret and Mackintosh often worked closely together on commissions for interior decoration. It was a marriage which was to give the volatile Mackintosh a life-long source of support and inspiration. He may have exaggerated her rôle in his work but he certainly always saw her as vital to it.

Mackintosh/MacNair Room for the Vienna Secession Exhibition, 1900, reconstructed by The Fine Arts Society, Edinburgh, 1983.

The Macdonald sisters had developed an enigmatic imagery of weird skeletal female figures and metamorphic lines owing something to Aubrey Beardsley, to the symbolism of Jan Toorop, and to the obscurer shadows of the Celtic Twilight. Their work earned the group the nickname 'The Spook School' and considerable suspicion of being tainted with the decadent influence of Art Nouveau. 'The Four's' first joint exhibition at the London Arts and Crafts Society in 1896 was hostilely received and Mackintosh was never able to outgrow this distrust of his early work in England. The achievements of his mature architecture and furniture design were virtually ignored.

On the Continent, however, 'The Four' were acknowledged as the most original of the Glasgow designers and as pathfinders in modern decoration. Their invitation to participate in the 8th Exhibition of the Vienna Secession in 1900 demonstrates the high regard they were held in by the Secessionists. Two years later an International Exhibition of Modern Decorative Art brought the designers of Europe together under the roof of Raimondo d'Aronco's highly ornate Pavilion in Turin, and amongst the extravagant excesses of continental Art Nouveau the restraint and clean-lined elegance of the Mackintosh/MacNair room caused a sensation. Mackintosh has so frequently been categorised as an 'Art Nouveau architect' that it is worth stressing the gulf between the firmly controlled, linear character of his work and the swirling, deliquescent style which treated wood, iron or stone as malleable plastic. As a friend remembered later: "Mackintosh didn't like Art Nouveau. He fought with these straight lines against these things like melting margarine."[2]

From Germany and Austria in particular Mackintosh received the acclaim that he was never to gain at home. The periodicals *Dekorative Kunst* and *Deutsche Kunst und Dekoration* published his work more frequently than the English *The Studio* and with fulsome praise. The Mackintoshes were fêted at Vienna where the success of their exhibit led to a prestigious Viennese commission and friendship with designers such as Josef Hoffman. The triumph at Turin was followed by invitations to exhibit at Dresden, Moscow and Berlin.

Mackintosh never received such recognition in his own country. What appeared to fellow architects and designers in Europe as outstanding, pioneering achievements were never taken quite seriously in Glasgow. Almost all his architectural work was created within a short period of intense activity between 1896 and 1909 and commissioned by just a handful of patrons and friends. Francis Newbery secured him the major commission to design the new Glasgow School of Art but this revolutionary building, a major landmark in the history of modern architecture, went almost unremarked. For Kate Cranston he designed the succession of famous Tea Room interiors, but their originality had no impact on Edwardian décor. The businessmen William Davidson and Walter Blackie commissioned large private homes, Windyhill and The Hill House, but Mackintosh's ideal of the total integration of architecture and interior design, involving his control of every detail of furniture and decoration, demanded too great a commitment on the part of the client and few were as sympathetic as Davidson or Blackie. Mackintosh could not bear to compromise, and commissions for clients who thought that they could modify his designs usually ended in the architect losing both his temper and his contract. In the years after the completion of the School of Art he achieved little save a few interiors for Miss Cranston.

By 1913 Mackintosh had given up hope of a viable architectural practice in Glasgow. He terminated his partnership with John Keppie and the next year he and Margaret accepted the Newberys' invitation to join them at their holiday home in Walberswick on the Suffolk coast. In all his holidays Mackintosh had sketched and painted profusely; now he absorbed himself in painting delicate watercolour flower studies which reveal his acute powers of observation. Seemingly there was a project, which the war made impossible, to publish these in a botanical text-book in Germany. It is also possible that he had received invitations from his continental friends to work in Ger-

"Blackthorn, Chiddingstone"
Watercolour, 1910
(Collection: Glasgow University)

"Fritillaria, Walberswick"
Watercolour, 1915
(Collection: Glasgow University)

Textile Design
Watercolour, c.1918
(Collection: Glasgow University)

8

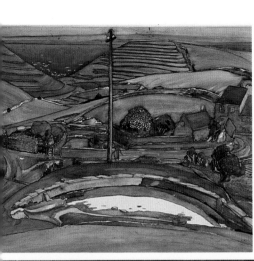

*"The Downs,
Worth Matravers"
Watercolour, 1920*
(Collection:
Glasgow School of Art)

*"Le Fort Maillert"
Watercolour, 1927*
(Collection:
Glasgow School of Art)

*"The Grey Iris"
Watercolour, c.1923*
(Collection:
Glasgow Art Gallery)

many or Austria. At any rate his correspondence aroused the suspicions of the war-time authorities against the incomer with an odd foreign accent and the habit of taking twilight walks after a day's painting: the unfortunate Mackintosh found himself arrested as a spy.

In 1915 Mackintosh and Margaret settled in Chelsea where he attempted to resume practice as an architect and designer. Mackintosh was deeply depressed at this time at the failure of his career, yet his creativity did not slacken in the least. The textile designs which he produced at this time and the interior schemes for 'The Dug-Out' Tea Room in Glasgow and No.78 Derngate in Northampton are not the products of a man wallowing in alcoholic self-pity (as he has too often been depicted) but astonishingly vigorous and innovative. The cool restraint of his earlier work is replaced by a dramatic new style, exploiting bold geometric motifs and vibrant primary colours. But the war made for a lean time for architects; most of his building projects were never executed, his beautiful still-life flower paintings did not sell, the extraordinary vitality and orginality of his designs went wholly unheeded in England. A solitary publication praised the Derngate interiors but omitted to mention the architect.

In 1923 the Mackintoshes moved again, this time to southern France where they settled first in Collioure and later in Port Vendres. Here Mackintosh finally abandoned all thought of architecture and concentrated entirely on watercolour painting. It was a time of relative poverty and obscurity, yet Mackintosh's letters from Port Vendres show him not depressed with his failure as an architect but utterly absorbed in mastering a medium that fascinated him. Architecture is never mentioned, yet the landscapes that he painted are themselves constructed with the eye of an architect: static, massive, concerned not with movement and light but with the formal relationship of man-made features imposed upon the natural patterns of the land. The forts that grow from the sheer rocks of the French cliffs are unmistakeably painted with the same hand and eye that raised the Glasgow School of Art.

In the summer of 1927 Margaret had to spend two months in London for medical treatment. Mackintosh's daily letters reveal not only his love for and dependence on her, but the gaiety and self-deprecating sense of humour that always endeared him to his friends, as well as his unaffected delight in the small things of the natural world.

By the end of the year Mackintosh himself was so ill with pain in the throat that he was forced to return to London and was treated for cancer of the tongue. He died on 10th December 1928, Margaret surviving him for five years. When she died the entire contents of their home and studio, including several of his chairs and the French paintings that he had been preparing for exhibition, were valued at £88.16s.2d.

The Guest Bedroom, 78 Derngate, 1919

The guest bedroom for Derngate, which Mackintosh redesigned in 1919, was even more dramatic in its decorations than the hall. The furniture was very plain, simple shapes in light oak trimmed with a narrow band of blue squares, but this was set against a wallpaper of black and white stripes, edged with bright blue, which covered the wall behind the twin beds and extended over them on the ceiling. The curtains and bedspreads matched the paper, with appliqué squares of blue and emerald green silk added to the stripes. It was Mackintosh's last design commission, and certainly his most daring and innovative.

Although Mackintosh did not leave behind him a great number of buildings, and achieved little recognition in his own country in his life-time, for many of his contemporaries on the Continent he was a pioneer and a genius. For the artists of the young Vienna Secession it was 'our leader' Mackintosh who 'showed us the way'; it was Mackin-

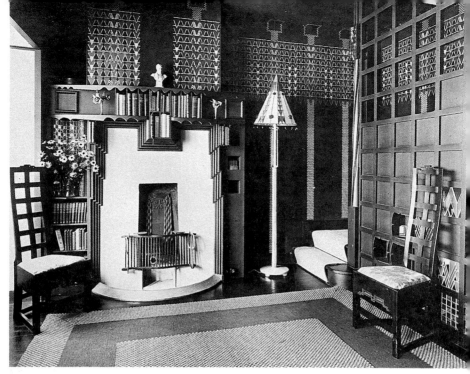

The Hall, No. 78 Derngate
Mackintosh decorated the very small hall of 78 Derngate with black
walls and ceiling and a dramatic stencilled wallpaper. The bold yellow
chevrons were echoed in panels of stained glass in the staircase screen,
and on the painted lampshade. All the furniture was painted black,
and based on a lattice of large squares.

tosh who Josef Hoffmann and Fritz Wärndorfer approached for ad-
vice on the establishment of the Wiener Werkstätte. About the same
time as he abandoned his failing practice in Glasgow, a gathering of
European architects and designers proposed the toast: "To our master
Mackintosh, the greatest since the Gothic". Despite his obscurity at
the time of his death, Mackintosh's obituary in *The Times*
acknowledged that "the whole modernist movement in European
architecture looks to him as one of its chief originators".

The conventions of Victorian architecture in which Mackintosh
was trained are demonstrated in his student designs for competitions:
a Greek public hall, a Renaissance Chapter House, a Gothic Railway
Station . . . It was this dependence on foreign historical styles which
had no relation to modern purposes that Mackintosh soon challenged:
"All great and living architecture has been the direct expression of the

needs and beliefs of man at the time of its creation. How absurd it is to see modern churches, theatres, banks, . . . made in imitation of Greek temples . . . There are many such buildings in Glasgow, but to me they are as cold and lifeless as the cheek of a dead Chinaman."[3]

Mackintosh was attacking the Glasgow establishment, but his outcry followed a lead already taken in England. J. D. Sedding had long since demanded: "No more museum-inspired work! . . . But instead . . . designs by living men for living men." Philip Webb, Shaw, Lethaby and other architects of the English Revival had established a well-respected domestic architecture based not on the 'museums' of Greece and Italy but on English traditions.

Like them, Mackintosh found his inspiration in the vernacular buildings of the countryside. It is the old cottages and details of village churches, and especially the Scottish castles and tower houses, that fill his sketchbooks and are the vocabulary of his architecture. All his buildings are deeply rooted in the past, they have the quality of belonging to, rather than being arbitrarily imposed upon the landscape that characterises vernacular architecture, yet Mackintosh's creativity is never hindered by nostalgia. He welcomed modern ideas and modern technology wherever he found them useful or attractive, exploiting to the full the machine-age innovations in plate-glass, steel and concrete and man-made materials. His interest was neither with revival nor with a rootless 'newness' for its own sake, but in creating an architecture truly relevant to the modern age that drew its strength from national traditions. In the buildings of the past he found not just the picturesque but a timeless, vigorous quality of unpretentious functionalism, a resilience to adaptation and change. "The newness of Mackintosh was the outcome of his instinct to design for practical requirements and give these decorative expression. That being his driving impulse he could not help being new in the result however many hints and suggestions he might have received from the past."[4]

Although he has often been described as a 'pioneer of the Modern Movement', the bold and exciting forms of Mackintosh's architecture and his totally original interior designs are far removed from the bleak utilitarianism of modernism. His concern was to build around the needs of people, people seen not as masses but as individuals who needed not 'a machine for living in' but a work of art.

1   Hermann Muthesius, "A Mackintosh Tea Room in Glasgow,"
    Dekorative Kunst, Vol. VIII, April 1905.
2   Ivor Davies and June Bedford, "Remembering Charles Rennie Mackintosh.
    A recorded interview with Mrs Mary Sturrock.",
    The Connoisseur, Vol. 183, No. 738, 1973.
3   Charles Rennie Mackintosh, Lecture on *Scotch Baronial Architecture* 1893.
4   Walter Blackie, "Memories of Charles Rennie Mackintosh,"
    Scottish Art Review, XI, No. 4, 1968.

THE MACKINTOSH HOUSE 1900, 1906

"There is no hope that our aesthetic cultural sense will prevail to allow such rooms to be accepted as normal. But they are milestones, erected, in anticipation, by a genius to demonstrate to mankind the higher and the sublime."[1]

FOR A VISITOR TO GLASGOW IN 1900 IT WAS A CITY OF dirty streets and smog-laden air, of houses that were blackened with grime outside and sombre with dark furnishings inside. It is no wonder that the experience of visiting the Mackintosh's flat was described with awe. Instead of the typically over-crowded Victorian sitting-room with its patterned wallpaper and dark upholstery, here was a room with plain white walls and a white carpet, where even the fireplace was whitewashed and the severe clean lines of the white furniture lacked drapes. By contemporary standards of comfort it must have seemed almost puritanically austere, the exquisite furniture—often appearing designed more for art than comfort—was sparse, the ornaments few and carefully chosen. There is an overwhelming impression of the debt that Mackintosh owed to the simple, yet infinitely subtle, interiors of Japan.

To live in Glasgow art circles in the late 19th century and avoid being influenced by Japanese art would have been difficult. The 'discovery' of Japanese art through the import of woodblock prints had left widespread trails of 'Japonisme' in western art, but Glasgow's links with Japan were particularly close. Clyde shipyards were building ships for the Japanese navy and training Japanese engineers; Christopher Dresser's visit to Japan in 1888 had resulted in a major gift of Japanese artefacts to the Glasgow Museum; the painters Henry and Hornel set out for their first tour of Japan in 1893, sponsored by the Glasgow art dealer Alexander Reid who imported Japanese prints . . .

Mackintosh's enthusiasm for 'things Japanese', however, went far beyond the woodblock prints and tea-bowls on his mantelpiece. The influence of Japan is as evident in his wrought-iron work and timber construction as it is in his flower-paintings and distinctive flower-arrangements, and in the sparsely-furnished, serene Japanese interiors Mackintosh found inspiration for his radically different approach to

"The whole world of interior decoration has been infinitely enriched by Mackintosh. Not only has he revealed new methods: he has upgraded their very concept". (Hermann Muthesius, 1904)

The Dining Room
In all his houses Mackintosh created rapid changes of atmosphere between one room and the next, and usually a sombre dining-room is contrasted with his bright white sitting- and bed-rooms. In his own dining-room he covered the lower part of the walls with a grey-brown wrapping paper, stencilled at intervals with a rose and lattice motif. Panelling and furniture is dark-stained and includes the distinctive dining-chairs which he originally designed for the Argyle Street Tea Rooms. The delicate oval backrails are pierced with a 'flying bird' motif and morticed into slender uprights—an unsympathetic treatment of wood which demonstrates how far Mackintosh had departed from the Arts and Crafts ideal of 'truth to materials'. Nonetheless the chairs have an almost sculptural elegance which makes them one of his best-known designs.

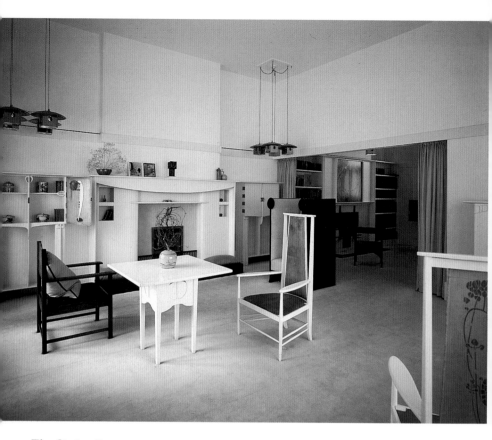

The Sitting Room
"On the second floor of a modest building in the great industrial smoky town of Glasgow there is a drawing room amazingly white."
(B. E. Kalas, 1905)

The inspiration of Japan pervades Mackintosh's own home, evident in the prints above the fireplace and the characteristic flower-arrangement, but also, more subtly, in the harmony and restraint of the decoration and the appreciation of the value of empty space—a concept remote from the 'horror vacui' of most Victorian interiors. By removing the wall between the sitting room and the studio Mackintosh allows the interiors to flow together, as they would in a Japanese house.

Mackintosh gave much more care to the comfort of the inhabitants of his rooms than he is usually credited with; the grey cushions either side of the fireplace were for the benefit of their two grey Persian cats.

Margaret seated at her writing desk in the Mackintosh's Main Street flat. (Photograph by J. C. Annan, c.1903)

interior design. The Japanese attitude to decoration was the antithesis to contemporary late Victorian and Edwardian taste. It valued restraint and economy of means rather than ostentatious accumulation, simple forms and natural materials rather than elaboration and artifice, the use of texture and light and shadow rather than pattern and ornament.

The traditional western distinction between 'fine art' and (inferior) 'crafts' is not made by the Japanese, to whom the flower arrangement and the vase are as much works of art as the painting on the wall, and all equally carefully chosen to harmonise with the whole design. Where the western interior is extrovert, intended to display the wealth and status of its owner in a multiplicity of objects, the Japanese room is a place of reflective calm, where both the paucity and quality of the

The Studio
"And in that lovely room with the white carpet Margaret Mackintosh put on white kid gloves and painted the gesso pictures that he used in his tea rooms." (Mary Newbery Sturrock, 1973)

In the window stands the handsome ebonised desk, decorated with mother-of-pearl chequers, which Mackintosh originally designed for Walter Blackie and replicated for his own use. One of Margaret's gesso panels hung above the fireplace.

Armchair with Stencilled High Back 1902 (Collection: Glasgow University)
Mackintosh exhibited this chair at the Turin exhibition in 1902, and several were made for the Music Salon in Vienna which he designed for Fritz Wärndorfer, the wealthy patron of the Vienna Secession group and an enthusiastic admirer of Mackintosh. The furniture which Mackintosh was designing at this time reveals his impatience with the traditional limitations of wood. Unlike the Arts and Crafts designers, his interest was not in craftsmanship or materials for their own sake, but in the visual impact of his furniture. The hard white enamel paint disguised the inadequate jointing of the delicate pieces and created the illusion that they were made from an entirely new material.

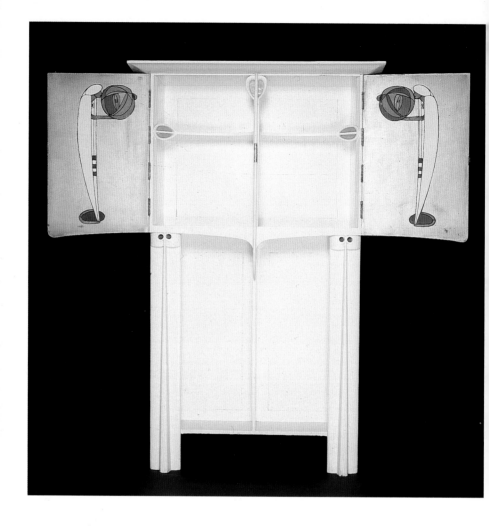

White Cabinet for 120 Mains Street, 1902 (Collection: Glasgow University)
"Every object which you pass from your hand must carry an outspoken mark of individuality, beauty and most exact execution"
(Charles Rennie Mackintosh, 1903)

Mackintosh designed two of these spectacular cabinets for his own flat, (a further two were executed for Mrs. Rowat), decorating the doors with unusual elaboration with his favourite motifs of stylised female figures and roses, executed in coloured glass on a silver ground.

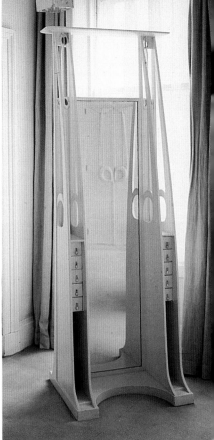

The Bedroom

"An almost mystical sense of peace is achieved by the wide surfaces. There is an impact of monumentality, broken only occasionally by a small, superimposed ornament. Its effect in turn is of a jewel".

(Hermann Muthesius, 1906)

For his own bedroom Mackintosh designed a four-poster bed, simple and massive in form, yet richly decorated with jewel-like insets of coloured glass and stencilled and embroidered hangings.

The cheval mirror for Mains Street is perhaps the most spectacular of several that Mackintosh designed, compared when first exhibited in Vienna to a great sledge placed on end.

Like the bed, the double wardrobe is severely plain in outline, but the severity is offset by the delightful carving of birds on the doors.

contents invite contemplation. Mackintosh absorbed all these ideas into his own work. He conceived each of his interiors as a unity, designing not merely the furniture but the wall-papers, carpets, lights, flower-vases, even fenders and fire-irons to create a room that is itself a work of art, which any addition or subtraction would mar.

When Mackintosh married Margaret Macdonald in 1900 he designed the interiors and furniture for their first home at 120 Mains Street, Glasgow. In 1906 they moved to the more fashionable area of Hillhead and converted an end house in Florentine Terrace (later Southpark Avenue), but the furniture from Mains Street came with them and the new rooms were decorated in a similiar fashion to the old. For Mackintosh's continental admirers, making their pilgrimage to 'grimy Glasgow' to see him, the house was something magical, an adventure not so much in interior design as in poetry. For Hermann Muthesius, who was principally responsible for publishing Mackintosh's work in Germany, the perfectionism of his rooms raised them right out of the realm of everyday use. "Their severe and at the same time subtle atmosphere cannot tolerate an intrusion of the ordinary . . . An unsuitably bound book on the table would be a disturbance. people of today . . . are strangers in this fairy-tale world."[1]

Yet to Mackintosh's and Margaret's friends, even if the house was 'strewn with the novels of Maeterlinck' and if Margaret's ability to paint on a white carpet *was* a mystery, it was also a welcoming home and place of cheerful company. Fra Newbery's daughter, a frequent visitor to the Mackintoshes, remembered: "the house was always so pretty and fresh. A bright red glowing fire, the right sort of cake, a nice tea, and kind hearts—and a lot of fun."[2]

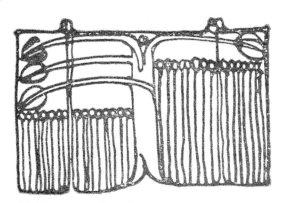

1 Hermann Muthesius on Mackintosh, 1904, reprinted in
   Scottish Art Review XI 1968.
2 Ivor Davies and June Bedford, "Remembering Charles Rennie Mackintosh.
   A recorded interview with Mrs Mary Sturrock."
   The Connoisseur, Vol.183, No.738, 1973.

GLASGOW SCHOOL OF ART

IT HAS BEEN ACCLAIMED AS A MAJOR LANDMARK OF THE
international Modern Movement, yet it is unequivocally Scots, a
descendent of medieval castles. For some it is an offshoot of Art
Nouveau; there are elements which are unmistakeably Japanese. It
has been condemned as resembling a workhouse or a prison. Some
have compared it with the achievements of Michelangelo.

At first sight it is austere, rectilinear, functional, its stark walls
stripped bare of sculptural ornament. Yet within and without functional glass and wood, metal and stone are conjured into decoration.
Austerity is relieved with a wilful asymmetry, straight lines break into
graceful curves, dark corridors open into white airy spaces. It stands
with one massive wall of stone planted squarely in Scotland's past and
another of glass leaping upward into the future: the Glasgow School
of Art.

THE
GLASGOW
SCHOOL
OF ART

IN 1896, WHEN HE WAS 28 YEARS OLD, MACKINTOSH ENTERED the competition to design a new building for the Glasgow School of Art. From the start it was a difficult and demanding commission. The site was narrow and extremely steep, the accommodation required extensive and, at the time the competition was announced, only £15,000 was available for the construction, equipping and furnishing of the entire building. It was an impossible project, and after considerable argument the Governors were reluctantly persuaded by the competing architects that only a portion of the School could be built for this sum.

The choice of Mackintosh's design was probably heavily manipulated by the Director, Francis Newbery. He knew the young architect well as one of his most outstanding and original students, and it is almost inconceivable that they had not discussed the needs of the new School together. Whatever persuasion Newbery had to use, the governors announced 'Honeyman and Keppie' as winners of the competition (Mackintosh, as mere draughtsman and not a partner in the firm, was rarely given any public acknowledgement) and work began in 1897.

Mackintosh had undertaken to build the eastern portion of the School, from the massive fortress-like wall on Dalhousie Street to the entrance hall with the Museum and Director's rooms above it, within the designated budget. This was opened in 1899 but it was not until 1907 that enough money had been raised to start construction of the western section. The time lapse spans the most productive and successful period of Mackintosh's life. During this time, Queen's Cross Church, Windyhill, The Hill House and Scotland Street School had been built; he had designed interiors and furniture for Miss Cranston's four tea-rooms and for her own home, exhibited at several international exhibitions and worked on many other commissions While he was working at such a pace, his ideas were changing rapidly and when he returned to the plans for the School Extension his original design for the west end was discarded for something much more adventurous. At the same time he added an attic story to the plans to provide extra studio accommodation, and stone staircases in each wing.

The North Facade 1897-99, 1907-09
"The north facade is one of the the greatest achievements of all time,
comparable in scale and majesty to Michelangelo."

(Robert Venturi, 1985)

Newbery's specification for the School had insisted on north-lit painting studios, and Mackintosh's huge plate glass windows, (reversing
the proportions of stone to glass usual in Victorian buildings) allow in
the maximum amount of light. The central 'tower' places the Director's rooms prominently in the heart of the building, but Mackintosh
avoids the obvious solution of axial symmetry either side of it: even
the size of the windows varies to reflect the different sizes of studio
within.

The studios in the top storey, added in the second stage of the
building, are slightly recessed from the main facade and almost invisi-
ble from the street.

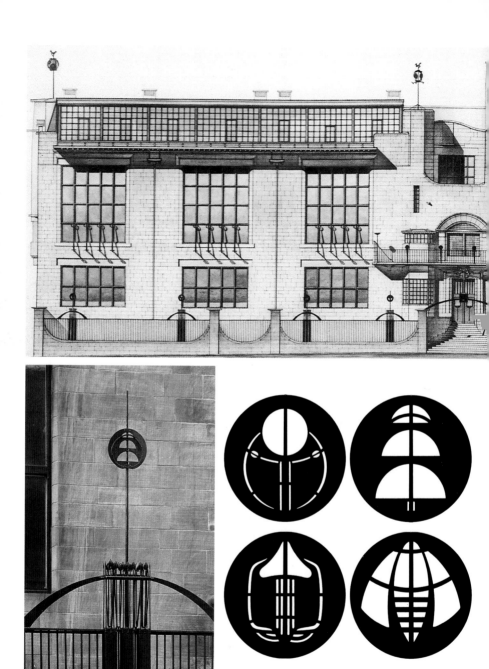

Francis Newbery,
Director of the Glasgow School of Art
1885-1918
Mackintosh owed his most important commission, the Glasgow School of Art, to the influence of 'Fra' Newbery, who remained a staunch supporter and friend throughout Mackintosh's life. A man of enormous energy and formidable personality, Newbery worked tirelessly for a new building worthy of the prestigious modern school that he was creating. It was his vision and determination that persuaded the governors to agree to Mackintosh's first unconventional design, and subsequently to his infuriatingly frequent changes of plan.

Wrought-iron Railings, North Facade
The decorative motifs on the iron railings can be read as stylised insects, bee, beetle and so on, but they also closely resemble Japanese 'Mon' or heraldic emblems.

Mackintosh and Newbery were determined that the School should be as well-equipped and modern as possible. Electricity was installed in 1899 and when it was completed the School had not only electric lighting but electric clocks in every studio and 'electric thrones' for the models. The building was heated by a sophisticated Plenum system which cleaned the air, warmed it and circulated it through the rooms by means of ducts in the walls.

Despite the limited budget, Mackintosh's design does not stop at making the School thoroughly functional. Somehow he coaxed joiners and plasterers, glaziers and blacksmiths (often against their will) to execute his seemingly inexhaustible invention of decorative detail; the interiors are worked out with a richness of imagination and care for not merely the convenience but the delight of those who would inhabit them.

Although retrospectively the Glasgow School of Art established Mackintosh as a 'Pioneer of the Modern Movement' and one of the greatest architects of his age, at the time it attracted astonishingly little comment. Apart from a few interior photographs in *The Studio* the School was not published in contemporary art journals, and the continental architects who were so impressed by illustrations of his tea rooms and domestic interiors had no opportunity to know of his greatest building. Glasgow seems to have taken its revolutionary new art school in its stride. The Governors congratulated themselves on their 'sound, substantial workmanlike building' and gave no credit to Mackintosh at all.

The East Facade 1897-99
"'Tis but a plain building that is desired"
(Governors of the Glasgow School of Art, 1897)

The sheer walls of the east wing rise gaunt and massive as a medieval fortress from the steep incline of Dalhousie Street, pierced by Mackintosh's distinctly random fenestration.

The governors' insistence on a 'plain building' was rewarded with a facade plain to the point of starkness in an age which regarded ornament as an essential part of architecture. Probably they were only persuaded to accept Mackintosh's extraordinary design because the radical lack of surface ornament made it cheap to build.

The windows to the right of the doorway were added in 1913 to give light to the Animal Room, where the students were given classes in drawing from live animals brought in from the menagerie of Hengler's Circus, then adjoining the School to the south. Isobel Stewart, who won her Art School Diploma in 1912, remembers an elephant, and a camel who banged its hump on the door and charged around the room in terror.

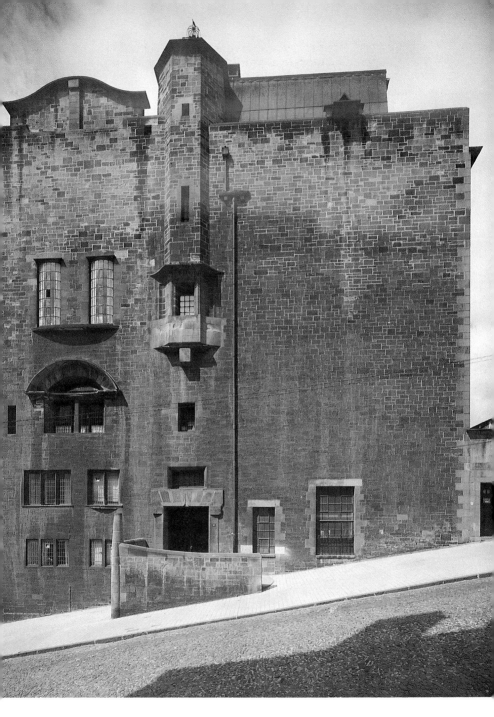

The South Facade 1897-1909

"Wayfarers stop and marvel that the authorities have permitted the running-up of a house of correction, or poor-house, on such a site."

(Building Industries, 1900)

It is not surprising that the southern facade provoked criticism. Small, irregular windows in wholly unornamented harled walls might be expected of dour vernacular buildings in the Scottish countryside, but hardly towering over one of Glasgow's chief thoroughfares. The severe elevation reflects no accepted 'style' of architecture but rather a pragmatic evolution in response to building needs. The conical-roofed staircase-tower in the eastern corner and the glazed corridor projecting from the attic floor were added in the second phase of the building, and did not form part of Mackintosh's original design.

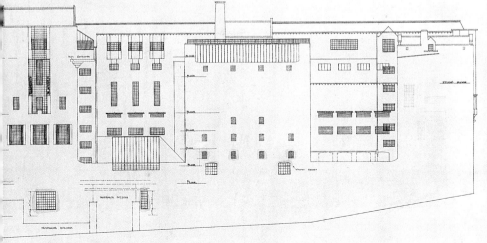

BACK ELEVATION

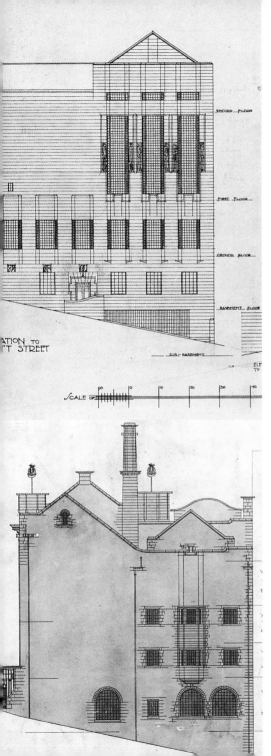

The West Facade
" . . . it appears to have no roof. Without cornice or ornamentation the walls stand stark bare as the pylons of the mosques of Ispahan."
(Hermann Muthesius, 1902)

In Mackintosh's first drawings for the School of Art the west end is much more conventionally treated, with relatively small windows on each floor. When he redesigned the extension in 1907 the elevation was radically altered, with oriel windows soaring through three storeys of the facade.

In the south wall the windows of the Library are incised, rather than projecting, so as not to detract from the impact of the west end. Mackintosh provides the studio on the top floor (originally the 'Composition Room') with a small glazed conservatory overhanging the sheer wall of the south facade—a modern version of the corbelled turrets on late medieval castles.

33

Detail of Library Windows
Mackintosh's drawings show that he originally intended the cylindrical blocks between the Library windows for figural sculpture (his notes mention Cellini and St. Francis but not, alas, the rest of his chosen pantheon). Presumably because the governors would not tolerate the additional expense, they were never executed.

Window Brackets on the North Facade
" . . . the extraordinary facility of our style in converting structural and useful features into elements of beauty"
(Charles Rennie Mackintosh)

Mackintosh's spectacular wrought-iron brackets, which functionally both brace the huge studio windows and support planks for the window-cleaners' ladders, also provide exciting decorative relief on the otherwise severe north elevation. The swirling patterns of the ironwork, evocative of basket-hilted swords, vary in each window.

The Director's Room 1897-99

In contrast to the dark-stained pine of the Museum and the corridors, the Director's room is bright and airy, lit by a large arched window and the panelled walls painted white beneath the projecting cornice. Newbery was provided with a handsome fireplace, generous built-in cupboards, his own cloakroom and even a hand-lift to bring up his letters from the office below. Above he had his own studio, with a trap door in the floor so that large canvases which could not be carried down the spiral staircase could be lowered on to the first floor. However, because the budget was so limited, Mackintosh designed very little moveable furniture for the School in the first building phase, and Newbery had to wait until 1904 for the table and chairs that were specially designed for this room.

The Main Entrance 1897-99

The strong linear emphasis of the main facade is broken by the gentle curve of the stone stairway, which sweeps outward to welcome the visitor up to the white front doors. The relief above the doorway is the only decorative sculpture on the building.

Detail of the Museum Roof

The Museum
The main stairway leads from the relatively dark entrance hall to the open space of the Museum in the centre of the School, top-lit by a glazed roof supported on four great timber trusses reminiscent of a medieval barn. Originally the Museum, now a temporary exhibition area, was filled with casts and examples for the students' drawing classes.

The Board Room 1897-99
Mackintosh intended this beautifully proportioned room, with its tall bow windows and magnificent granite fireplace, for the Governors' Board Meetings. For lack of space in the unfinished School, the room was used as a design studio and a smaller Board Room provided in the second stage of the building. It has now reverted to its original purpose and also houses the large pieces of furniture and light fittings designed for Windyhill and donated to the School by the Davidson family.

Students working in the Museum, c.1900

Linen Cupboard for Gladsmuir, 1896
The green-stained wood and decorative brass strap hinges are
characteristic of Mackintosh's earliest pieces of furniture which were
clearly influenced by the English Arts and Crafts designers, especially
C. A. Voysey.

Light Fitting from Windyhill, 1901
The light fitting from the stairway at Windyhill is one of several spectacular designs in steel and coloured glass made for Mackintosh's
interiors.

Bookcase from Windyhill, 1901
Almost more sculpture than bookcase, the massive form and simple
lines are reminiscent of traditional oak furniture, but the kimono
shape is uniquely Mackintosh.

41

The Board Room, 1906
The Governors apparently thought their original Board Room too bright and frivolous for its serious purpose. Mackintosh accordingly made the new room dark-panelled and suitably sombre and teased the governors with a thoroughly irreverent treatment of classical columns.

Detail of Wooden Panelling, Board Room

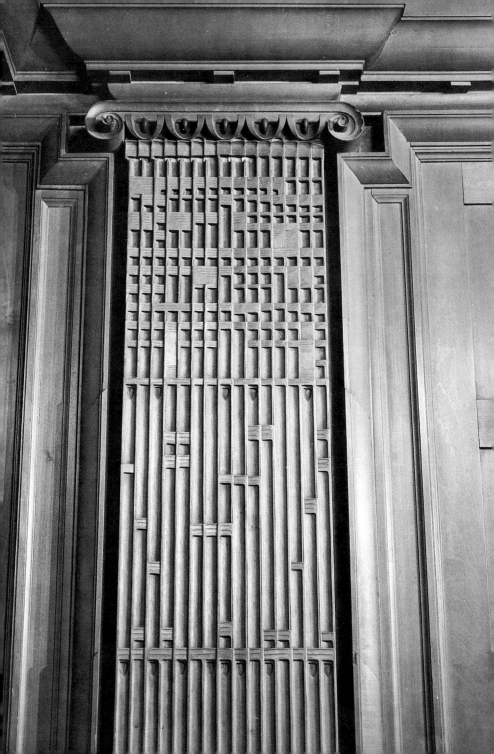

The Library, 1907-09

The great three-storey windows of the west wall and a central fall of lights like a giant mobile of miniature skyscrapers illuminate the School Library, Mackintosh's most celebrated and spatially exciting interior. Split beams carry the weight of the gallery to the main columns, and the space between column and gallery is decoratively filled with wagon-chamfered posts picked out in red, green and white: Mackintosh's earliest use of primary colour which becomes a salient feature of his later work. The openwork gallery pendants are an elaboration of an idea he had used in Queen's Cross Church ten years earlier, but here the 'abacus' motif varies in each pendant and in each repetition on the table and periodical desk legs.

Periodical Desk for the Library, 1910

The West Staircase, 1907-09
The narrow stone stairways in the wings with their arched openings in the stair well are finished with decorative ironwork at the top storey. A 'portcullis' and 'yett' of iron reinforce the impression of being inside a medieval castle.

Central Light Fitting in the Library, 1909

The East Staircase, 1907-09
The stone staircases in the east and west wings were not part of the original design, but added in the second phase of construction for fire safety. Mackintosh's theory that architecture should faithfully reflect stages and changes in building use is seen here: instead of removing the blocked-off windows of the Board Room he simply fits the stairway round them.

Wall Clock for the School of Art

Finial of the East Tower
Mackintosh designed several versions of the Glasgow coat of arms in ornamental ironwork for the School. The bird, bell and tree are all references to miracles performed by St. Mungo, the patron saint of Glasgow.

THE HILL HOUSE

"Here is the house. It is not an Italian Villa, an English Mansion House, a Swiss Chalet, or a Scotch Castle. It is a Dwelling House."[1]

WITH THESE WORDS MACKINTOSH HANDED OVER THE newly built The Hill House to its owner, the publisher Walter Blackie. It was the third dwelling house that he had designed in the first few years of the 20th century. Windyhill in Kilmacolm was built for his friend William Davidson in 1901 and in the same year the much larger and more elaborate Art Lover's House was designed for an international competition organised by Koch, the publisher of *Deutsche Kunst und Dekoration*. Although this house was never built, it was published as a portfolio of colour lithographs and so just as influential in disseminating Mackintosh's ideas on the Continent as Windyhill or The Hill House, which were both well illustrated in the German periodicals.[2]

The plan and facades of The Hill House closely followed those of the Art Lover's House, which Muthesius had described as "exhibiting an absolutely original character . . . unlike anything else known".[2] However, despite the 'modern' features such as the flat roof of the sun-lounge and staircase 'tower', there are in the massive chimneys of The Hill House and its pepper-pot angle-tower, in a certain uncompromising solidity in the plain harled walls with their small windows, unmistakeable signs of a long Scots ancestry.

Mackintosh's pride in "the architecture of our own country, just as much Scotch as we are ourselves"[3] is evident in all his buildings, but this is much more than an insular nationalism, or mere nostalgia for the picturesque. There is a world of difference between his practical use of vernacular precedent and the romantic revivalism characteristic of many of his English contemporaries, such as Voysey and Baillie Scott, which led them to reproduce olde-worlde medieval features with all the gross inconveniences of medieval planning. Mackintosh's quarrel with the imitative styles of architecture in which he had been trained was not just that the styles were 'foreign' but that they imposed upon a building a preconceived facade quite regardless of its purpose; what appealed to him in vernacular buildings was their no-nonsense functionalism. Internal planning was allowed to evolve naturally around a family's needs, windows were placed in walls where they were useful from the inside, rather than where they conformed to symmetry on the outside.

It is this emphasis on a house's *use* rather than its ornamentation that characterises Mackintosh's domestic architecture. He already knew the Davidson family well when he built Windyhill and when Blackie approached him with the commission for The Hill House he asked to be allowed to spend some days with his family, so that he could get to know them and build their home around them, from the inside out. When he began work, it was the interior plans that he sub-

Perspective Drawing of The Hill House from the South-West by Charles Rennie Mackintosh, 1903 (Collection: Glasgow School of Art)

It is interesting to see from Mackintosh's drawing that he originally designed figural sculptures to decorate the stone "shutters" flanking the bedroom windows. As with the sculptures designed for the west wall of the School of Art, these were removed in the final plans: Blackie may have thought them too costly or felt that the fussy element detracted from the strength of the otherwise simple facade. The striking feature of the projected battered chimney rising from ground-level at the west gable gives prominence to the main entrance.

mitted first for approval, and only when these had been agreed upon that he designed the elevations. The priorities of Mr. Blackie were given consideration with the provision of a library off the entrance hall so that he could entertain business visitors without their entering the family rooms, and a bedroom at the furthest end of the house from that of his children! For the children there was a delightful alcove on the first floor with a raised floor, ideal for games and theatrical performances. (Mackintosh had already included such a feature at Windyhill for the Davidson children, to whom he was 'Uncle Tosh' and a favourite stand-in for Santa Claus; despite the apparent severity of his all-white interiors he loved children and certainly took their needs as well as those of their elders into account).

Blackie was evidently thoroughly impressed with the care that Mackintosh took over the smallest details of his house. "To the larder, kitchen, laundry etc he gave minute attention to fit them for practical needs, and always pleasingly designed. With him the practical purpose came first. The pleasing design followed of itself . . . Every detail, inside as well as outside, received his careful, I might say loving, attention."[1]

Blackie could not afford new furniture for every room (he may well not have wished to sacrifice all his existing effects in the interests of 'total design'!) but he was extremely sympathetic to Mackintosh's ideals and allowed him a free hand to order the total furnishing and

The Hill House from the South East
The main rooms of the house overlook the garden and the Clyde, with the flat-roofed sun-lounge projecting from the sitting-room onto the terrace. Mackintosh attempts to soften the awkward junction between the three-storey service wing and the main block with a traditional pepper-pot angle-tower, echoed in the garden shed disguised as a dovecot below.

Perspective Drawing of The Hill House from the North-West by Charles Rennie Mackintosh, 1903   (Private Collection)

decoration of the hall, library, drawing-room and principal bedroom. Mackintosh had already had the opportunity to work out his ideas for domestic interiors in his own flat at 120 Mains Street, at Windyhill and in the Art-Lover's House designs, and his interiors for The Hill House are some of his most accomplished and sophisticated.

Mackintosh was never again to enjoy such a good relationship with his clients as he had with the sympathetic William Davidson and Walter Blackie, who both remained loyal friends. Blackie was to write later:

"During the planning and building of The Hill House I necessarily saw much of Mackintosh and could not but recognise, with wonder, his inexhaustible fertility in design and astonishing powers of work. Withal, he was a man of much practical competence, satisfactory to deal with in every way, and of a most likeable nature."[1]

1   Walter W. Blackie, *Memories of Charles Rennie Mackintosh* 1943, reprinted in *Scottish Art Review* XI 1968
2   Hermann Muthesius, Introduction to *"Meister der Innenkunst, Charles Rennie Mackintosh, Glasgow: Hans Eines Kunstfoundes"* (Darmstadt, 1902).
3   Charles Rennie Mackintosh, Lecture on *Scotch Baronial Architecture,* 1891.

Detail of Hall Light

The Hall

The spacious hall is furnished as a reception room, with a fine fireplace and table and chairs of a simple and sturdy design. The walls are alternately panelled with strips of dark-stained wood and grey-brown paper, stencilled with an abstract pattern, the coloured glass of the magnificent light fittings showing to advantage against the dark decor.

The Sitting Room

Mackintosh made the L-shaped sitting room into almost two distinct
rooms, with an additional bay containing the grand piano separated
from the main space. At the 'summer' end, a long window projects into the garden, furnished with window seat and book racks. The
'winter' end focuses on the fireplace, decorated with an elaborate
mosaic fire-surround and Margaret's gesso panel above it.
Characteristically, Mackintosh has no cornice separating wall and
ceiling (originally probably painted dark red) which are continuous
above a moulding running round the room at doorway height. Below
the moulding the white walls are stencilled with a design of roses and
chequers in pink and green and silver.

Detail of Sitting Room Light and Wallpaper

Another of Mackintosh's magnificent steel and coloured glass light fittings hangs in the stairway at The Hill House.

Landing Recess on the Stairway
The recess on the stair landing is characteristic of the way Mackintosh plays with the effect of light and shadow as light is broken by an open screen, like sunlight falling through trees—a typically Japanese device.

The Bedroom

The master bedroom of The Hill House was probably the most successful of the several white bedrooms that Mackintosh designed. An L-shaped room like the sitting room, a barrel vault over the bed separates the sleeping alcove from the main area of the room with fireplace and couch. Walls, ceiling and furniture are painted white, punctuated by the stark black of the two delicate little ladderback chairs and touches of pink in the fabrics and insets of coloured glass in the wardrobes and fireplace. The furniture is a more sophisticated version of that designed for the Windyhill bedroom (now in the Glasgow School of Art collection), the wash-stand in particular much more elaborately decorated with the striking abstract pattern on the splash-back.

Music Room from An Art Lover's House (Collection: Glasgow School of Art)

Mackintosh's designs for the Art Lover's House competition were his one opportunity to design his 'ideal home' unfettered by the demands of real clients or the limitation of real budgets. The exterior is very similar to The Hill House, but on an even larger scale, and the interiors are decorated with an extravagance that probably none of Mackintosh's Glasgow clients could have coped with. The Art Lover's elegant

Music Room is lit by tall windows all along one side, the vertical emphasis repeated in the attenuated female figures stencilled in the recesses, the clusters of coloured lamps suspended on slender wires and the exaggeratedly high-backed chairs. The effect of restless brilliance culminates in the fantastic superstructure of the piano.

Windyhill, 1901

Mackintosh designed Windyhill, Kilmacolm for his friend William Davidson in 1900. The Davidson family sold the house in 1918, but preserved the furniture, most of which is now housed at the Glasgow School of Art.

64

THE
TEA
ROOMS

"It is not the accent of the people, nor the painted houses, nor yet the absence of Highland policemen that makes the Glasgow man in London feel that he is in a foreign town and far from home. It is a simpler matter. It is the lack of tea-shops."[1]

THE GLASGOW TEA ROOM WAS A NEW SOCIAL phenomenon of the 1880s, thought to have no parallel outside Glasgow and for whose comforts the Glasgow man would pine in vain when away from his native city. It was an amenity ardently promoted by the Temperance Movement, whose determined crusade to provide counter-attractions to gin-shops was so successful that tea rooms sprang up in every corner of the city, and fears were expressed for the effects of over-indulgence in tea . . .

"In the old days . . . to frequent a public house demanded of a man a certain inclination towards licence, a certain disregard of propriety . . . Nowadays the very innocence of the liquid purveyed in the tea shop is the devil's own device for soothing the conscience of the strictly bred. They enter, thinking no evil, and at the end issue as tea-sodden wretches that are worse than drunkards."[1]

Despite such misgivings, the tea rooms played a vital rôle as places of refreshment, meeting-places and, with a peculiarly Glasgow sensibility that 'tea and beauty should go together', as art galleries. Many of the 'Glasgow Boys' paintings first saw the light of day in a Glasgow restaurant.

It was Miss Catherine Cranston who saw both the social need and the commercial possibilities of something more than a mere restaurant. Starting with a single tea shop, she created a veritable empire of tea rooms that gave an entirely new connotation to the word. Tea Rooms in the Cranston style were social centres of no mean order. There were rooms for ladies only and for gentlemen only, and rooms where both sexes could dine together; there was a reading room, a billiards room for the gentlemen and a smoking room where they could relax over coffee and dominoes. To Miss Cranston's came business men and apprentices, ladies and ladies' maids with democratic appetites. The service was impeccable and the food (older

Miss Catherine ('Kate') Cranston   (Photograph by J. C. Annan)

Glaswegians remember nostalgically) superb and the décor was quite unlike anything anyone had seen before.

"It is believed that in no other town can you see in a place of refreshment such ingenious and beautiful decorations in the style of the new art as in Miss Cranston's in Buchanan Street."[1]

The decorations were by Mackintosh and the Buchanan Street murals his first commission from Miss Cranston and the beginning of a twenty-year partnership. The small commission for Buchanan Street in 1896 was followed by another for furniture for the Argyle Street Tea Rooms the following year, and in 1900 for the White Dining Room at the Ingram Street Tea Rooms. These were conversions of existing premises, but in 1903 Mackintosh was given the sole commission for the design and decoration of a new building for Miss Cranston's final venture, the Willow Tea Rooms.

In Kate Cranston Mackintosh found his ideal client. She was not only an astute businesswoman but shared his vision of bringing art into every aspect of daily life and into everyone's reach. When he was failing to gain work anywhere else in Glasgow she was always willing to pioneer his most innovative designs: the blue 'Chinese Room' added to Ingram Street in 1911 is the first example of Mackintosh using bright primary colour on a large scale, and this was followed up by the dramatic almost Art Deco interiors for 'The Dug-Out' in 1917. Like Mackintosh, she was a perfectionist, perhaps even more of one. Mackintosh would have agreed with Voysey's dictum: "cold vegetables are less harmful than ugly dish-covers, one affects the body and the other affects the soul"; Miss Cranston would have tolerated neither alternative. Between them they raised the tea-room business from mere commerce into an art form.

The Willow in Glasgow's fashionable Sauchiehall Street was the most ambitious and elegant of the four tea-rooms. Given complete control, Mackintosh was able to unify the scheme of decoration, which throughout is based on the theme of willows ('Sauchiehall' means 'alley of willows'), expressed in stylised form in the furniture, stained glass and a frieze of plaster panels. There was nothing too trivial for Mackintosh's attention; every detail of the decor, furniture and fittings was designed by him or Margaret, down to the last flower-vase, menu or teaspoon.

It was typical that Mackintosh's utterly original interiors should receive far less publicity at home than abroad. Almost a whole issue of *Dekorative Kunst* was devoted to the illustration and appraisal of the Willow Tea Rooms which were virtually ignored in British journals. Hermann Muthesius, the author, lamented Mackintosh's unrewarded struggle to "hold up the banner of Beauty in this dense jungle of ugliness."[2]

"Miss Cranston, whose tea-rooms, designed by Mr. Mackintosh, are reckoned by some of the pilgrims to Glasgow as one of the sights of the city."   *(The Studio, 1902)*

Something of Kate Cranston's considerable personal panache is conveyed in the multi-layered dress and crinoline of the 1850s in which she cut such a distinctive figure in Edwardian Glasgow.

Sir Edwin Lutyens (who found Buchanan Street "just a little outré") left a rather less flattering portrait than Annan's of her. He wrote to his wife from the tea-room "Miss Cranston is now Mrs. Cochrane, a dark, fat wee body with black sparkling luminous eyes, wears a bonnet garnished with roses, and has made a fortune by supplying cheap clean goods in surroundings prompted by the New Art Glasgow School."   (Edwin Lutyens, 1898)

"Glasgow is a very Tokio for tea-rooms. Nowhere are such places more popular and frequented."   *(Glasgow in 1901)*

"Greens, golds, blues, white rooms with black furniture, black rooms with white furniture, where Whistler is worshipped and Degas tolerated."   (Edwin Lutyens)

1 James Hamilton Muir, *Glasgow in 1901*.
2 Hermann Muthesius, "A Mackintosh Tea Room in Glasgow," *Dekorative Kunst*, April, 1905.

The Willow Tea Rooms, 1903

At the Willow Mackintosh was able to design the architecture as well as the interiors. The facade has been restored almost as he designed it to be.

Mackintosh contrasts delicate, slender ladderbacks with squat, boxy armchairs in the main saloons and gallery of the Willow Tea Rooms, the dark-stained oak furniture standing out against the white paint.

He often intended his furniture to have an architectural or sculptural function within an interior: here his famous Willow settle, the lattice construction making a pattern of a stylised willow in the back, originally acted as a room divider between the white front and dark back saloons, as well as providing a seat for the manageress. She apparently had a system for conveying orders by dropping colour-coded balls down a tube to the kitchen in the basement.

The Front Saloon, the Willow Tea Rooms

"The chairs is no' like ony ither chairs ever I clapped eyes on, but ye could easy guess they were chairs; and a' roond the place there's a lump o' looking-gless wi' purple leeks pented on it every noo and then." (Neil Munro: *Erchie in an Art Tea Room*)

"Today any visitor to Glasgow can rest body and soul in Miss Cranston's tea rooms and for a few pence drink tea, have breakfast and dream that he is in fairy land." (Hermann Muthesius, 1905)

"If I cannot be graceful and comely, I can at least have a graceful and comely umbrella, and so help to keep up my interest in those qualities." (C. A. Voysey)

The Gallery,
the Willow Tea Rooms

The Room de Luxe,
the Willow Tea Rooms

The most precious of Mackintosh's tea-rooms, and definitely the most up-market place for ladies to take afternoon tea, the purple and silver interior of the Room de Luxe originally sparkled in the light from a huge Mackintosh-designed chandelier, reflected in the frieze of mirror-glass above the purple stretched-silk panels. Opposite the fireplace, a gesso panel by Margaret Mackintosh illustrated the Rossetti sonnet "O ye, all ye that walk in Willowwood" and the leaded mirror-glass carries the willow theme around the walls and across the window. The Room de Luxe (restored with reproduction furniture in 1983) is the only one of Miss Cranston's tea-rooms where one can still have tea.

Chair and Table for the Room de Luxe
(Collection: National Museums for Scotland) and (Collection: Glasgow School of Art)

All the furniture for this room was painted silver, the chairs upholstered in purple velvet and chair-backs and table-legs decorated with insets of lilac glass that matched the stretched-silk panelling around the walls.

*Mackintosh's most elaborate design in stained glass, the doors to the
Room de Luxe repeat the theme of stylised willows, and his favourite
motif of the rose.* (Photograph by Douglas Corrance)

Waitresses in the Room de Luxe

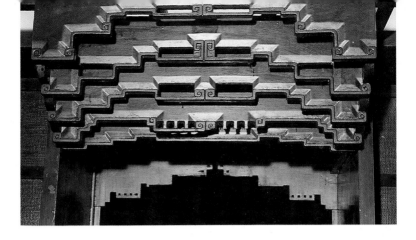

Detail of Lintel in the Chinese Room

The Tea Rooms gave Mackintosh a latitude for light-hearted fantasy that was not possible in his more serious commissions. The 'Chinese Room' was separated from the rest of the building and the mundane world by a lattice screen of bright blue with pagoda finials and cloud-form lintels, and furnished with a 'Chinese' cash desk and light fittings of a particularly exotic design.

The Chinese Room, Ingram Street Tea Rooms, 1911
(Partially reconstructed at Glasgow Museums and Art Galleries)

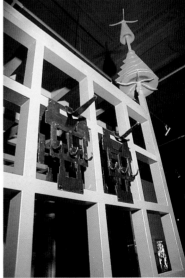

MISS CRANSTON'S

191 BUCHANAN STREET

SPECIAL AFTERNOON TEA SERVED IN WHITE ROOM FROM THREE O'CLOCK

MUSIC ON TUESDAYS AND THURSDAYS DURING WINTER MONTHS FROM 4 TILL 7

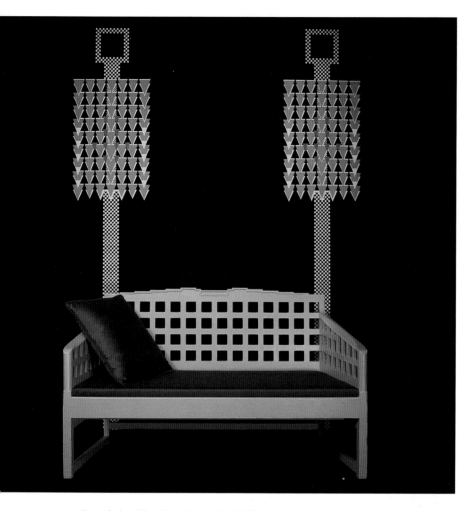

Couch for The Dug-Out, the Willow Tea Rooms, 1917. The wallpaper in the background is a reproduction of Mackintosh's designs for Derngate, page 12.

(Collection: Glasgow School of Art)

Mackintosh's last commission for Miss Cranston developed the dramatic new style of decoration he had employed in the Derngate interiors the preceding year. 'The Dug-Out' was a war-time conversion of basement rooms in the Willow: walls and ceiling were painted black enlivened by touches of blue and emerald green and two chrome-yellow couches with purple upholstery.

QUEEN'S
CROSS
CHURCH

WHEN HIS FIRST DRAWINGS FOR THE GLASGOW
School of Art had been accepted, Mackintosh's next architectural
commission was for a church at Queen's Cross, Glasgow. The site was
rather cramped on the junction of two main roads, and Mackintosh
had the problem of giving his church a sense of monumentality to
compete with the tall tenement blocks that then surrounded it. He attempted to solve this with sturdy proportions and a distinctive tower,
strengthened with angle-buttresses, at the corner. Mackintosh would
often rework details of vernacular buildings that appealed to him into
his own architecture, and the tower of Queen's Cross with its unusual
batter, the octagonal crenellated turret and the angle-buttresses are all
features lifted directly from a Somersetshire church in Merriot that
Mackintosh sketched on one of his holidays.

The interior is simple and spacious, with Mackintosh's hand
everywhere evident in the characteristic motifs of stylised birds or
plant forms carved into the pink stonework of the piers or the wooden
panelling of the chancel walls and furniture. Also characteristic of
Mackintosh is the homage to 'exposed construction' somewhat brutal-
ly expressed in the steel tie beams which cut across the arched timber
roof.

Clearly he was experimenting at Queen's Cross with decorative
ideas which he developed further in later commissions. The openwork
pendants in the gallery balustrade, for example, are his first working
of an idea to be used with such skill in the School of Art Library ten
years later.

The wooden panels of the pulpit are carved with a characteristic
design of stylised birds and leaves. Mackintosh re-uses a vocabulary
of favourite motifs again and again in his work: the oval panel at the
back of the pulpit is reminiscent of his oval back-railed chairs designed
for the Argyle Street Tea Rooms, while the split-circle motif in the centre had already occurred in the roof-beams of the Museum in the
School of Art.

St MATTHEWS CHURCH GLASGOW

CHARLES R MACKIN

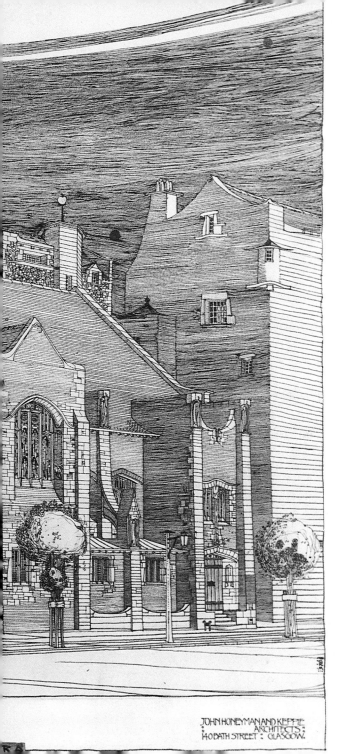

Mackintosh's
Design for
St. Matthew's
Church
(now Queen's
Cross Church)
1897.
(Collection:
Glasgow University)

JOHN HONEYMAN AND KEPPIE
ARCHITECTS
140 BATH STREET : GLASGOW.

The Nave

SCOTLAND
STREET
SCHOOL

MAKINTOSH'S LAST PUBLIC COMMISSION WAS FOR Scotland Street School, completed in 1906. A rigorously symmetrical, functional red sandstone building, the dominant feature of the main facade is the pair of semi-circular staircase towers with their immensely tall windows. Mackintosh's treatment of these towers typifies his inventive use of traditional architecture: staircase bays with conical roofs often occur in Scottish domestic architecture, but he has given them a 'modern' look by reversing the usual balance of wall and window, so that the stonework is pared to slender mullions in walls of glass.

The plan of the School is simple, a central classroom block with entrances for Girls and Boys (strictly segregated) in the base of the towers, and another door for the Infants in the middle. With a nice touch of humanity, Mackintosh scales down this doorway in comparison to the others, so that the architecture does not overwhelm the smallest inhabitants.

In his original design the facade was made much more lively by the use of smaller and more varied window panes but, as usual, Mackintosh was working to a limited budget and the windows were considerably simplified in the final execution. The south facade, overlooking the playground to the rear, is severely simple and uniform, the only decorative interest the carved stonework, with a pattern of green chequers, framing the end windows.

The
North Facade

*Detail of Windows
on the South Facade*

CHRONOLOGICAL TABLE OF MACKINTOSH'S LIFE AND PRINCIPAL WORKS

1868   Charles Rennie Mackintosh born in Glasgow

1877   Entered Alan Glen's High School, Glasgow

1884   Apprenticed to John Hutchison, Architect
Commenced evening classes at the Glasgow School of Art

1889   Joined John Honeyman & Keppie, Architects
Awarded Queen's Prize at South Kensington; several School prizes; Glasgow Institute's Design Prize.

1890   Awarded Alexander Thomson Scholarship
Awarded National Silver Medal, South Kensington
First commission: 'Redclyffe'

1891   Scholarship tour of Italy

1892   Awarded National Gold Medal, South Kensington

1893   Glasgow Herald Building Tower
Interior details for the Glasgow Art Club
Interior details for hall and library, Craigie Hall
Furniture for David Gauld

1894   Queen Margaret's Medical College

1895   Martyrs' Public School
Furniture for Guthrie & Wells

1896   Glasgow School of Art building competition
First commission for Miss Cranston: mural decorations for Buchanan Street Tea Rooms
Furniture and stencil decorations for Gladsmuir for William Davidson

1897   Design for Glasgow School of Art accepted; work began on east wing
Furniture for Argyle Street Tea Rooms and Gladsmuir
Queen's Cross Church
Music Room for Craigie Hall

1898   Ruchill Church Hall
Dining-room for H. Brückmann, München
Bedroom for J. Maclehose at Westdel, Glasgow
1901 Glasgow International Buildings Competition (unexecuted)

1899   Furniture for Glasgow School of Art
Furniture for Queen's Cross Church

1900	Married Margaret Macdonald
	Furniture and interiors for own flat, 120 Mains Street, Glasgow
	Furniture for Dunglass Castle, Bowling
	The White Dining Room, Ingram Street Tea Rooms
	Room for 8th Exhibition of the Vienna Secession
	Windyhill for William Davidson
1901	Furniture for Windyhill
	The Daily Record Office, Glasgow
	Gate Lodge, Auchenbothie
	An Artist's Town House & Country Cottage projects (unexecuted)
	An Art Lover's House competition (unexecuted)
	Stands at International Exhibition, Glasgow
	Furniture and interiors for 14 Kingsborough Gardens, Glasgow for Mrs Rowat
1902	Rooms for International Exhibition of Modern Decorative Art, Turin
	Music Salon for Fritz Wärndorfer, Vienna
1903	The Willow Tea Rooms
	The Hill House for Walter Blackie
	Liverpool Cathedral competition (unexecuted)
	Exhibition room, Moscow
	Exhibition room for the Dresdener Werkstätten für Handwerkskunst
1904	Became partner in the firm: Honeyman, Keppie & Mackintosh
	Scotland Street School
	Furniture and interiors for Hous'hill for Miss Cranston
	Furniture for The Hill House
	Furniture for the Glasgow School of Art
	Chancel furniture for Holy Trinity Church, Bridge of Allan
1905	Dining-room for A. S. Ball, Berlin
	Furniture for Abbey Close Church, Paisley
1906	Elected Fellow of R.I.B.A.
	Moved to 78 Southpark Avenue; new interiors and furniture
	The Dutch Kitchen, Argyle Street Tea Rooms
	Moss-side, Kilmacolm for H. B. Collins
	Auchenibert, Killearn for F. J. Shand
	The Board Room, the Glasgow School of Art
1907	Redesigned Glasgow School of Art west wing, attic storey added
	The Oak Room, Ingram Street Tea Rooms
	Additions to The Moss, Dumgoyne

1908	Alterations to Lady Artists' Club, 5 Blythswood Square, Glasgow
1909	Card Room for Hous'hill
	Oval room and Ladies Rest Room, Ingram Street Tea Rooms
	Interiors for west wing, Glasgow School of Art
1911	Cloister Room and Chinese Room for Ingram Street Tea Rooms
	White Cockade restaurant for Miss Cranston
1913	Left Honeyman & Keppie
1914	Moved to Walberswick, Suffolk; painted watercolour flower studies
1915	Moved to Chelsea
1916	Furniture and interiors for 78 Derngate, Northampton for W. J. Bassett-Lowke
	Fabric designs for Messrs. Foxton and Messrs. Sefton of London
1917	The Dug-Out, the Willow Tea Rooms
	Clocks for Bassett-Lowke
1918	Furniture and decorations for Candida Cottage for Bassett-Lowke
1919	Guest bedroom for 78 Derngate
	Cottage at East Grinstead for E. O. Hoppe
1920	Studios in Chelsea
	Studio flats for the Arts League of Service (unexecuted)
	Theatre for Margaret Morris (unexecuted)
1923-27	Lived in Port Vendres, southern France and concentrated on landscape painting.
1928	Mackintosh died in London of cancer of the tongue.

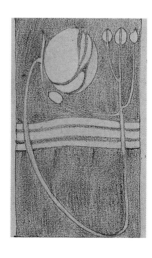

F. Alison, *Charles Rennie Mackintosh as a Designer of Chairs*
(London 1974)
H. Jefferson Barnes, *Some Examples of Furniture by Charles Rennie
Mackintosh in the Glasgow School of Art Collection* (Glasgow
1968)
Some Examples of Metalwork at the Glasgow School of Art
(Glasgow 1868)
R. Billcliffe, *Architectural Sketches and Flower Drawings by
Charles Rennie Mackintosh* (New York 1977)
Mackintosh Watercolours (London 1978)
*Charles Rennie Mackintosh: The Complete Furniture, Furniture
Drawings and Interior Designs* (London 1979, 3rd ed. 1986)
Mackintosh Textile Designs (London 1982)
Mackintosh Furniture (London 1984)
R. Billcliffe and P. Vergo, "Charles Rennie Mackintosh and the
Austrian Art Revival" *Burlington Magazine* CXIX, 1977, pp.739-46
D. P. Bliss, *Charles Rennie Mackintosh and the
Glasgow School of Art* (Glasgow 1961)
J. Cooper, *Mackintosh Architecture, The Complete Buildings and
Selected Projects* (London 1978)
T. Howarth, *Charles Rennie Mackintosh and the Modern Move-
ment* (2nd ed. London 1971)
G. and C. Larner, *The Glasgow Style* (Edinburgh 1979)
A. McLaren Young, *Architectural Jottings by Charles Rennie
Mackintosh*, Glasgow Institute of Architects, (Glasgow 1968)
R. Macleod, *Charles Rennie Mackintosh, Architect and Artist*
(2nd ed. London 1983)
A. Macmillan and Yukio Futagawa, *Charles Rennie Mackintosh,
The Glasgow School of Art, Glasgow, Scotland, Great Britain
1887-99, 1907-09* (Tokyo 1979)
N. Pevsner, "Charles Rennie Mackintosh", *Studies in Art,
Architecture and Design* II (London 1968)
Scottish Arts Review XI, no.4 1968 (Special number devoted to
Mackintosh)

The Studio IX 1897, pp.203-05 (Arts & Crafts Exhibition 1896)
        XI 1897, pp.86f, 226f (Buchanan Street Tea Rooms; furniture)
        XIX 1900, pp.48f (Glasgow School of Art)
        XXIII 1901, pp.237f (Glasgow International Exhibition 1901)
        XXVI 1902, pp.91f (Turin International Exhibition 1902)
        XXVIII 1903, pp.283f (Ingram Street Tea Rooms)
        XXXIX 1906, pp.31f (Argyle Street Tea Rooms)
The Studio Special Number 1901 (Mains Street interiors)
The Studio Year Book of Decorative Art 1907 (The Hill House; Hous'hill)

Clock for The Hill House

EXHIBITIONS OF WORK BY CHARLES RENNIE MACKINTOSH

Charles Rennie Mackintosh, Margaret Macdonald Mackintosh,
Memorial Exhibition, McLellan Galleries, Glasgow 1933
Charles Rennie Mackintosh, Saltire Society and Arts Council
Exhibition, Edinburgh 1953
Charles Rennie Mackintosh: Architecture, Design and Painting,
Edinburgh Festival Exhibition 1968
Le Sedie di Charles Rennie Mackintosh, Triennale di Milano,
Milan 1973
Flower Drawings by Charles Rennie Mackintosh, Hunterian Art
Gallery, Glasgow 1977
Charles Rennie Mackintosh 1869-1928, Art Gallery of Ontario,
Toronto 1978
Mackintosh Watercolours, Glasgow Museums & Art Galleries and
The Fine Arts Society, Glasgow 1978
Charles Rennie Mackintosh: The Chelsea Years 1915-23, Hunterian
Art Gallery, Glasgow 1978
Charles Rennie Mackintosh Designs 1868-1928, Seibu Museum of
Art, Tokyo 1979
Some Designs by Charles Rennie Mackintosh, The Architectural
Association, London 1981
Lost Furniture Found, Glasgow School of Art 1982
Charles Rennie Mackintosh, Kunstindustriemuseen, Copenhagen
1982; Helsinki 1983
*Vienna 1900: The Scottish Room for the Eighth Exhibition of the
Vienna Secession, A Reconstruction,* The Fine Arts Society,
Edinburgh 1983
The 1933 Memorial Exhibition, A Reconstruction, The Fine Arts
Society, Glasgow 1983
Margaret Macdonald Mackintosh 1864-1933, Hunterian Art
Gallery, Glasgow 1983
Charles Rennie Mackintosh, Architect and Designer 1868-1928
(Thomas Howarth Collection) Federal Reserve Board Building,
Washington D.C. 1985
Charles Rennie Mackintosh, Glasgow School of Art and the Japan
Art and Culture Association, Tokyo, Sendai and Osaka 1985-86

Queen's Cross Church, 870 Garscube Road, Glasgow G20 7EL
(041-946 6600)
As a result of the demolition of the surrounding tenement buildings, it
ceased to be a congregational church in 1976. Since 1977 it has been
the headquarters of the Charles Rennie Mackintosh Society, who
have been responsible for its maintenance and repair. Open Tuesdays,
Thursdays, Fridays 1200-5.30pm, Sundays 2.30-5.00pm.

Glasgow School of Art, 167 Renfrew Street, Glasgow G3 6RQ
(041-332 9797)
Still an art school, but certain rooms are open to the public with a
substantial collection of Mackintosh furniture, paintings and designs
on display. Guided tours only, Mondays-Fridays 10.00-12am,
2.00-4.00pm.

Mackintosh House, Hunterian Art Gallery, University of Glasgow,
University Avenue, Glasgow G12 (041-339 8855)
The house at 78 Southpark Avenue, where Mackintosh and Margaret
lived from 1906 until 1913, was demolished in 1963, but the principal
interiors were reconstructed around the original furniture and fittings
in the new wing of the Hunterian Art Gallery, opened in 1981. The
gallery also houses the reconstructed Derngate guest bedroom and the
largest collection of Mackintosh's drawings and watercolours.

The Hill House, Upper Colquhoun Street, Helensburgh (0436 3900)
Walter Blackie's family lived in the house until 1953 and sold it with
most of the furniture designed by Mackintosh. It is now owned by The
National Trust for Scotland and open daily 1.00-5.00pm.

The Willow Tea Rooms, 271 Sauchiehall Street, Glasgow G20
(041-331 2569)
The only one of Miss Cranston's tea rooms to survive, the Willow was
restored in 1979/80 and is leased to M. Henderson, Jewellers. The
Room de Luxe on the upper floor was re-opened as a tea-room, with
reproduction Mackintosh furniture, in 1983. Open normal shopping
hours.

Glasgow Museums & Art Galleries, Kelvingrove, Glasgow G3 8AG
(041-357 3929)
The permanent Glasgow Style gallery includes the reconstructed
Chinese Room from the Ingram Street Tea Rooms and other works by
Mackintosh. Open Mondays-Saturdays 10.00am-5.00pm. Sundays
2.00-5.00pm.

Scotland Street School, Scotland Street, Glasgow (041-429 1202)
Due to the demolition of the surrounding housing area, it closed as a
School in 1979 but is administered by the Strathclyde Region Education Department as a Museum of Education. Appointment necessary
to visit.

Ruchill Church Hall, Ruchill Street, Glasgow G20
Open Tuesdays, Wednesdays, Thursdays 10.30am-3.30pm